BABYLON'S DAUGHTERS

THE LEGACY OF
SEDUCTION IN THE NATIONS

DAMIANO B. CENTOLA

EXPLORA BOOKS
700 – 838 West Hastings St. Vancouver, BC V6C 0A6
www.explorabooks.com
Phone: (604) 330 6795

Because of the dynamic nature of the Internet, any web addresses or links contained in this book may have changed since publication and may no longer be valid. The views expressed in this work are solely those of the author and do not necessarily reflect the views of the publisher, and the publisher hereby disclaims any responsibility for them.

Bible verses are quoted from the King James Version (KJV), which is public domain, the English Standard Version (ESV), and the New King James Version (NKJV).

ISBN: 978-1-997587-85-9 (Paperback)
978-1-83430-048-1 (Hardback)
978-1-83430-010-8 (eBook)

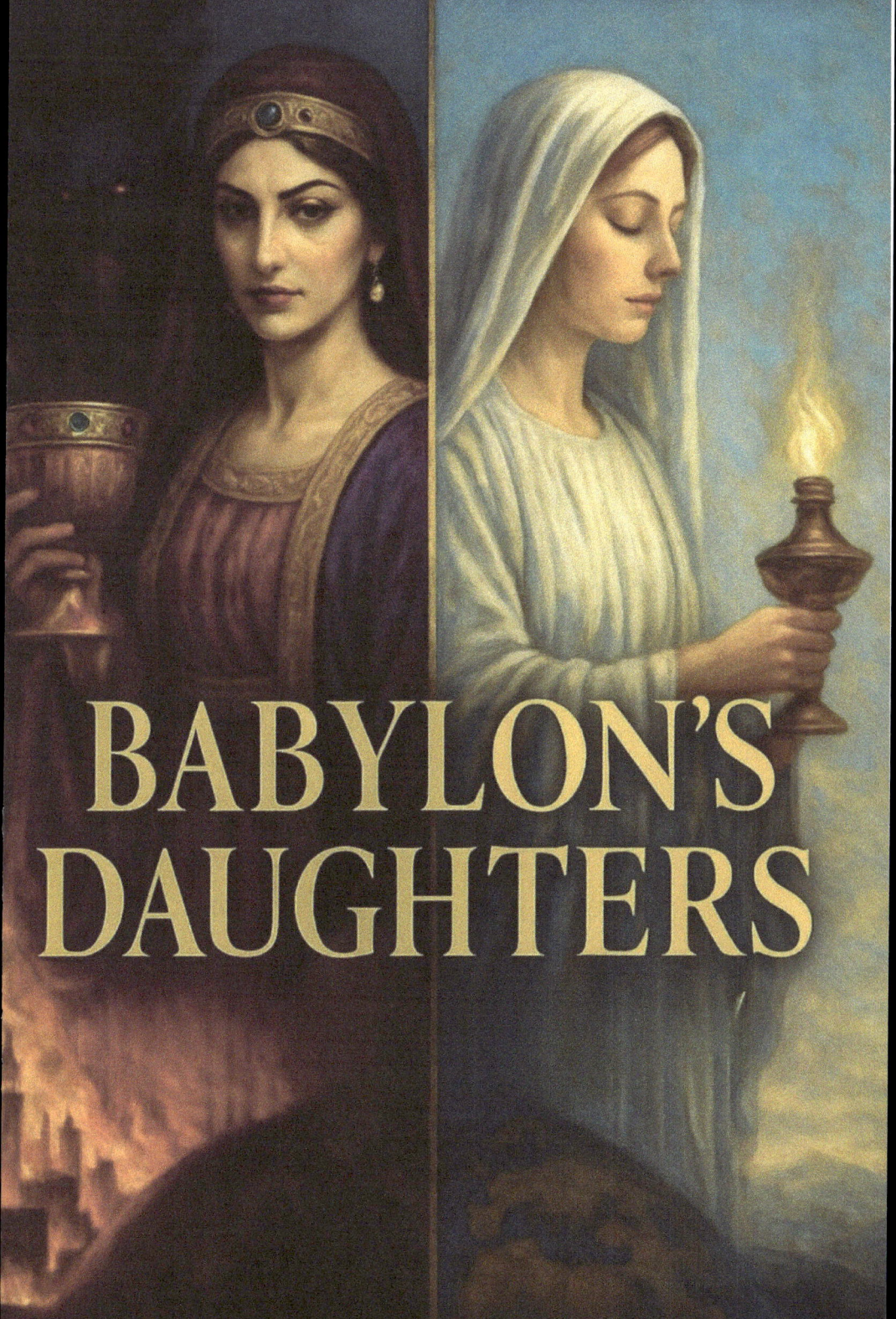

BABYLON'S DAUGHTERS

Table of Contents

Preface
From the book: Babylon's Daughters — The Legacy of Seduction in the Nations

There are some spirits that do not die when empires fall.

The name "Babylon" has echoed through history, not merely as a city, not only as an empire, but as a spiritual infection. Her buildings crumbled. Her throne was buried. Her merchants moved on. But her daughters multiplied.

This book is not about ancient Babylon. Nor is it simply about the judgment already prophesied in Revelation. That judgment has been written. Her smoke will rise. Her fall is guaranteed. This is not a warning of what is coming — it is an unveiling of what is still active. This is a book about what remains.

Though Babylon has fallen, her spirit remains enthroned in systems that call themselves holy, in churches that have traded the Gospel for gold, and in governments that pretend peace while dealing in the blood of the innocent. Her voice speaks from pulpits and boardrooms. Her daughters sit at every table where compromise, corruption, and spiritual adultery are served.

The world may no longer call her "Babylon," but her perfume still lingers. Her theology still sells. Her cup is refilled daily in songs of false unity, in celebrity gospel, in altars of mixture where the fire no longer falls.

This book is the third in a prophetic trilogy — beginning with The Mother of Prostitutes, deepened in The Mother of Harlots, and declared with finality in The Fall of Babylon: The Blood of Saints and the Cry from the Earth. But now, in this work, I turn to the residue. To what remains after the collapse. To the daughter spirits — the subtle, surviving strains of Babylon's seduction still infecting nations, denominations, and even hearts.

This book is a trumpet. It is a warning. And it is a call.

Not all who name the name of Christ belong to the Bride. Not all who preach the Cross are free from the harlot's influence. This is a message to the remnant. To those who are willing to be purified. To those who will not bow to mixture. To those who will follow the Lamb wherever He goes.

The Spirit of the Lord is saying once again:

> *"Come out of her, My people."*

This is not the end of Babylon's story. It is the end of her influence — if we will choose truth.

This book is written with trembling. It is written in the fire of the altar and in the shadow of the Blood. May it pierce where it must. May it awaken what is sleeping. May it call forth the bride — watching, waiting, and without spot.

Let the daughters of Babylon be named.

And let the bride arise.

–Damiano B. Centola

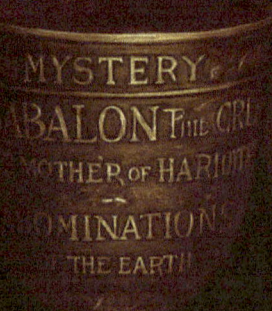

Chapter One
Babylon's Bloodline: The Harlot Has Daughters

She was never meant to survive.

Her judgment was written before the foundations of the earth.

And yet — she does.

Not in name, but in nature.

Not in body, but in blood.

The woman in scarlet, seated upon the beast, drunk with the blood of the saints — she is not gone. She has merely multiplied.

What began with Babel and culminated in Babylon did not disappear in the ashes. It passed on a spiritual DNA — a bloodline of seduction, deception, and domination — to those who would carry her name without wearing her crown.

She has daughters now.

The Anatomy of a Harlot System

In Revelation 17, John sees a woman — mysterious, majestic, and terrifying. She rides upon many waters, clothed in purple and scarlet, adorned with gold, pearls, and precious stones. But in her hand is a cup. Not of righteousness. Not of truth. A cup full of abominations and the filth of her fornication.

And upon her forehead is written:

"Mystery, Babylon the Great,
The Mother of Harlots and Abominations of the Earth."
(Revelation 17:5 KJV)

She is not just a harlot. She is the mother of them. She births systems. She breeds spiritual adultery. She spawns cities and churches and governments that drink from her cup and speak with her tongue.

And this is the mystery:

Though her fall has begun, her daughters still reign.

The Birthright of Rebellion

Her daughters are not born in innocence. They are born in rebellion. Babylon, from the beginning, was a tower — a declaration that man could reach Heaven on his own terms. A unity without God. A religion without truth. A kingdom without righteousness.

This spirit — of self-exaltation, of mixture, of compromise — was the womb from which her children came.

She gave birth to Rome — an empire of brutality and spectacle.

She whispered to Greece — offering wisdom without repentance.

She sat beside Germany in the cathedrals that burned books and people alike.

She walked into America, wearing freedom's name but selling slavery's chains.

But her most dangerous children are not the empires.

They are the ones who look holy, but carry her secrets.

Hidden in the Pulpit, Thriving in the Pew

The daughters of Babylon are not always easy to see.

They wear white robes. They sing worship songs. They quote

scripture — but they drink from her cup.

When the Gospel is diluted in exchange for applause —

a daughter speaks.

When churches sell truth to partner with kings — the harlot grins.

When prophets prefer platforms over purity — Babylon gives

them favor.

When worship becomes entertainment, and holiness becomes

optional — her bloodline is alive and well.

She teaches her daughters well.

They do not preach seduction — they live it.

They do not deny the Cross — they decorate it.

A Seduction in the Name of Unity

What makes her legacy most dangerous is this: she seduces through

false peace. She offers unity, ecumenical alliances, interfaith bridges,

and coexistence banners — all at the cost of truth.

She whispers:

"Let us all be one. Forget doctrine. Forget repentance.
Forget holiness. Let love win."
But it is not the love of Christ she offers — it is the
counterfeit affection of compromise.

Babylon's daughters are building a church without Christ, a kingdom

without a King, a spirituality without the Spirit.

And millions are drinking from her cup — believing it to be

communion.

The Call to Discern

To expose this bloodline is not to walk in judgment, but in discernment.

It is not to accuse, but to separate.

The Bride of Christ is being purified. The false church is being revealed.

And every soul must now choose:

Will you be a daughter of Babylon, or a child of Zion?

There is no neutral ground in the end.

Closing Reflection

The Harlot has daughters.

They sing louder. They shine brighter.

But their light is false.

Their fire is strange.

Their wine is poison.

And their time is short.

The Spirit is calling — to the prophets, to the watchmen, to the remnant —Unmask the daughters. Call out the bloodline. Raise the banner of righteousness again.

Babylon may fall in one hour.

But until that hour comes, her daughters preach.

And we must answer.

Chapter Two
She Sits in the Shadows: The Spirit That Lingers After the Fall

She no longer rides the beast in plain sight.

She sits in shadows now — behind pulpits, within governments, under robes, behind veils. Her name may no longer be written in stone, but her spirit is etched in the architecture of modern religion and the soul of global systems.

Babylon has fallen — and yet, she is everywhere.

How can something so judged still influence so much?

Because spirits do not die like cities.

They linger.

And those who do not discern them become their hosts.

The Spirit of Babylon Is Not a Myth

Many believe that Babylon is merely a symbol — a metaphor for Rome, for ancient empires, for bygone evils. But Babylon is more than a place. She is more than a moment. She is a spirit.

She is the spirit of pride, building towers in the name of progress.

She is the spirit of mixture, blending truth with error to make it more appealing.

She is the spirit of false religion, where appearance replaces holiness.

She is the spirit of control, where kings and priests hold hands for profit.

Babylon's architecture is spiritual — and so her legacy is unseen. You can tear down her buildings, but if you don't tear down her altars in the heart, she remains enthroned.

Where Does She Linger?

She lingers where truth is inconvenient.

She sits where purity is mocked.

She thrives where righteousness is expensive and compromise is cheap.

Let us not be naïve — Babylon has found a new home in:

- Churches that mirror entertainment industries instead of upper rooms.
- Pastors who wear her fragrance but speak the name of Jesus.
- Governments that trade human dignity for economic gain.
- Movements that shout justice but deny repentance.

She sits, not on a beast now, but on platforms, on screens, and in the hearts of the undiscerning.

When Jezebel Rebrands Herself

There was a time when Jezebel painted her face and ruled from a palace. But when she was thrown from the wall and her body devoured by dogs, her spirit did not die. It passed on — like a corrupted inheritance — and has now merged with the seductions of Babylon.

Together they form a powerful counterfeit:

Jezebel controls the prophetic

Babylon corrupts the priesthood

Both silence the true voice of God with noise, glamour, and fear

And the tragedy? Many who once cast out demons now host them, because they do not recognize their new appearance.

The Language of the Harlot

The spirit of Babylon does not shout — she seduces. She speaks in tongues of inclusivity, love without truth, and spirituality without submission.

Her phrases sound noble:

"We're all God's children."

"God is doing a new thing — forget the old."

"Don't judge. Just love."

"Doctrine divides. Unity unites."

"Jesus hung out with sinners, so we must too — without preaching righteousness."

These are not always lies. But in her mouth, they become weapons.

She weaponizes compassion to kill conviction.

She uses mercy as a mask to hide manipulation.

She has learned how to preach Jesus without the Cross,

how to offer power without holiness,

and how to draw crowds without calling them to repent.

This is not revival. This is Babylon's liturgy.

Why the Spirit Remains

One may ask — why hasn't God fully removed her yet?

Because God will never destroy what His people are still willing to host.

The Lord is patient. He sends warnings. He raises prophets. He stirs discernment. But if the church will not cast her out, Babylon will continue to sit — dressed in robes of glory — while drinking the blood of saints.

She remains because she is invited.

And she will not leave until the Bride makes herself ready.

A Holy People Must Arise

The presence of Babylon's daughters is not a cause for despair — it is a call to action.

The Church must be:

Discerning, not gullible

Holy, not trendy.

Consecrated, not compromised.

Prophetic, not performative.

We are not called to dialogue with the Harlot — we are called to cast her down.

Final Reflection

She sits.

She smiles.

She sings songs that sound like worship.

But she is not the bride.

Babylon is not finished because the Church has not fully renounced her.

But she will fall — again.

And her daughters will burn.

Because the One who comes with eyes like fire will not share His Bride with another.

Let the fire begin in the house of God.

Let those who sit with her rise and flee.

For soon, the shadows will be exposed.

And only one woman will remain — clothed in white, pure, watching, and ready.

Chapter Three
The Cup Is Refilled — False Worship in the House of God

She once drank from it alone.

Now, she has taught others to pour.

The golden cup in her hand, filled with abominations and the filth of her fornication (Revelation 17:4), is not empty.

It is refilled.

By preachers.

By prophets.

By worship leaders.

By nations who sing songs to Heaven but walk with the Harlot.

And the tragedy?

They lift the cup in the name of Jesus.

Worship Without Holiness

Worship is sacred. It is the incense of Heaven, the fragrance of surrender, the echo of angels and saints.

But Babylon has infected it.

What was once holy has become a spectacle.

Lights replace the lampstand.

Sound replaces silence.

Emotion replaces repentance.

Atmosphere replaces anointing.

And applause replaces the presence of God.

In many houses of worship today, Jesus is referenced,

but not reverenced.

Songs are sung about Him, but few speak to Him.

The Bridegroom is no longer the focus — the performance is.

And Babylon watches…

Smiling.

Drinking.

Clapping with the crowd.

The Abomination of Mixture

The golden cup in the harlot's hand is not filled with poison alone.

That would be easy to detect.

It is a cup of mixture — part truth, part lie; part Spirit, part flesh.

She has taught worshippers to:

Sing about holiness, while tolerating sin.

Declare freedom, while remaining in bondage.

Offer praise with lips, but keep idols in their hearts.

This is the most dangerous form of deception — when the sound of Heaven is copied, but the fire never falls.

"Like Nadab and Abihu, many offer strange fire today..."
(Leviticus 10:1–2 KJV)

It looks like devotion.

It smells like praise.

But it is not received.

Babylon's Music Ministry

Make no mistake — the spirit of Babylon has a music ministry.

She knows how to write songs that move emotions but never pierce the soul.

She funds productions that stir the flesh but never break the heart.

She trains artists to market worship like a product — not offer it like a sacrifice.

She does not mind the sound of worship — as long as it does not lead to repentance.

And so the cup is passed...

Through playlists.

Through concerts.

Through conferences.

Through Sunday morning sets that stir the body but never convict the spirit.

The wine tastes sweet — but it is fornication with her name on the label.

The Cry of the Levites

Where are the true Levites?

Where are the ones who tremble before touching the Ark?

Where are the musicians who fast, weep, and consecrate themselves before they play a note?

Worship is warfare — not entertainment.

It is sacrifice — not production.

It is for an audience of One — not a room of thousands.

The Levites in David's day carried the Ark on their shoulders, not with carts made by Philistines (1 Chronicles 15:13–15).

But today, we let Babylon build our platforms, design our lights, coach our voices — and then wonder why no glory descends.

It is not because God has changed.

It is because the cup has changed hands.

False Fire at the Altar

"When Solomon dedicated the Temple, the fire of God fell from Heaven and consumed the sacrifice..."
(2 Chronicles 7:1 KJV)

There was no question that God was present.

But now, we light the fire ourselves.

We simulate the glory.

We manufacture the tears.

And we wonder why the heavens remain silent.

Babylon's daughters know how to mimic power.

They have studied revival.

They've read the manuals.

They've learned the language.

But they have not been broken.

And so the altars are filled — but the sacrifices are unclean.

The Cup or the Cross?

There is always a choice at the altar.

A choice between the cup of Babylon or the cup of Christ.

One is sweet and easy.

The other is bitter and holy.

Jesus prayed, "Father, if it be possible, let this cup pass from Me..." (Matthew 26:39 KJV)

That cup was the cost of obedience.

Babylon offers a different one — filled with applause, acceptance, pleasure, pride, and deception.

And every worshipper, every church, every generation must choose:

The cup of compromise or the cup of covenant.

A Call to Purify the Worship

Let the prophets speak.

Let the musicians weep.

Let the platforms be torn down.

Let the pulpits be purged.

It is not too late.

The fire can still fall — but only if the cup is cast down.

Only if worship is reclaimed.

Only if we once again tremble before the Holy.

Final Reflection

She has refilled the cup.

But the Lord is calling Levites again.

He is raising up singers whose sound comes from the secret place — not from Spotify.

He is calling worshippers who sing barefoot, broken, and burning.

Let the false altars fall.

Let the harlot's music cease.

Let Zion arise with harps in hand and swords in mouth.

And let the glory return.

The Beast She Rides

Chapter Four
From Rome to Wall Street — Global Thrones of Seduction

Babylon's empire was never just territorial — it was ideological, spiritual, and systemic.

> *"She was not content to sit upon a single throne. She desired many waters — the tongues, nations, tribes, and kings of the earth..."*
> *(Revelation 17:15 KJV)*

Her strategy was not war by sword but influence by seduction. She reigned through luxury, intimidation, manipulation, and compromise.

And when one empire fell, she simply shifted thrones.

From Rome to London, from Berlin to Washington, from the Vatican to Silicon Valley, from Alexandria's libraries to Wall Street's trading floors — Babylon has passed her cup from hand to hand, throne to throne, pulpit to parliament.

She has built herself a global seat of power, and her daughters now reign from it.

Babylon Never Dies — She Reinvents

Every generation has believed they were free from Babylon — and every generation has fallen prey to her modern mask.

Rome was her throne of empire.

The Vatican became her throne of religious control.

Europe gave her science without God.

America gave her wealth without wisdom.

And now, the global web of technology and finance has become her newest beast.

She does not need to conquer cities when she can conquer cultures.

She does not need a crown when she has screens and contracts.

The New Babel: The Seduction of Global Unity

In Genesis 11, the Tower of Babel was a warning:

> *"Let us build... let us make a name... lest we be scattered..."*

It was not just a structure — it was a vision of globalized man-made unity, a system that bypassed obedience to God in favor of collective control.

That vision is alive again — dressed in diplomacy, diversity, and digital harmony.

But at its core is the same seduction:

Unity without truth

Progress without holiness

Peace without the Prince of Peace

This is Babylon 2.0 — and her daughters sit in powerful seats:

Financial cartels that trade nations like pawns.

Media empires that preach false gospels.

Education systems that indoctrinate rather than teach.

Political unions that declare humanism as god.

All built on her blueprint. All serving her agenda.

All leading to confusion, the very meaning of her name.

The Merchants of the Earth Are Drunk

Revelation 18 is clear:

> *"The merchants of the earth have become rich through the abundance of her delicacies..." (Revelation 18:3 KJV)*

Babylon's system is not only spiritual — it is economic.

She has made kings and corporations rich.

She has made preachers wealthy and prophets silent.

She has built kingdoms that call themselves democracies but behave like dictatorships — so long as the harlot's commerce flows freely.

Wall Street is not evil in itself.

Rome was not evil in itself.

But when these thrones become vessels for the Harlot's agenda — trading souls for stocks, truth for influence, children for ideologies — then they become part of her daughters' empire.

And judgment is not far behind.

Thrones in the Church

Let us not forget — the Harlot does not only sit in secular places.

She has built thrones inside the sanctuary.

Thrones of celebrity pastors.

Thrones of prosperity gospel kings.

Thrones of apostolic networks built for profit.

Thrones of Christian influencers more loyal to culture than the Cross.

And the danger? These thrones look like ministry — but they are Babylon's design.

She does not fear the Church.

She builds within it.

Come Down, O Thrones of Compromise

There is a cry rising in the Spirit:

> *"Come down, O thrones of seduction.*
> *Be cast into the dust, you altars of mixture.*
> *Let the righteous rule in holiness again!..."*

The only throne that will remain is the one in New Jerusalem — and the only government that will endure is the Kingdom of our God.

Every other system — no matter how powerful, polished, or global — will fall.

A Remnant Must Rise

You are not called to bow to the thrones of this age.

You are not called to sit at Babylon's table.

You are not called to preach in her cathedrals or dance in her sanctuaries.

You are called to overturn tables,

to tear down high places,

and to declare that the Kingdom of God is not for sale.

Final Reflection

From Rome to Wall Street, from cathedral to conference, from political summit to spiritual stage — the Harlot has built her empire.

But it is shaking.

The wind is rising.

The Lion is roaring.

And those who reign with her will fall with her.

Let every false throne be cast down.

Let every seductive system be unmasked.

Let the Spirit cry out again:

> *"Come out of her, My people."*
> *"For her thrones are dust,*
> *but Zion's throne is eternal..."*

Chapter Five
Prophets Who Sleep with Jezebel —
Modern Mixture in the Church

There was a time when prophets stood alone.

They were torn by the word of the Lord, weeping between the porch and the altar. They feared no king, bowed to no culture, and wept when the people laughed. Their garments were not polished. Their voices were not popular. But Heaven knew their names.

Now, in this generation, the prophets eat at Jezebel's table.

And worse — many of them sleep in her bed.

The Spirit of Jezebel Is Alive in the Prophetic Movement

Jezebel is not just a name from 1 Kings.

She is a spirit of corruption that invades the prophetic to pervert it.

"She loves influence more than intimacy.
She loves control more than consecration.
She loves to be called "prophetess" — but hates
repentance..." (Revelation 2:20 KJV)

She seduces with:

   Flattering words.

   Spiritual credentials.

   Half-true visions.

   Marketed revelations.

And ministries built more on charisma than on the Cross.

And tragically, many who were once pure vessels have now traded their mantle for visibility.

They still prophesy. But the oil is gone.

When the Prophetic Becomes Professional

The true prophetic is birthed in fire, in brokenness, in the weight of the Lord's burden.

But Babylon and Jezebel have joined forces to turn it into a career path.

Prophetic schools sell impartations for a fee.

Webinars and masterclasses replace weeping and fasting.

Personal prophecy booths offer "encouragement" with no accountability

Conferences feature profit-seeking prophets who prophesy only blessings, never warnings.

They say, "Peace, peace," when there is no peace.

They speak visions from their own heart.

They trade accuracy for applause, and truth for popularity.

And Babylon funds it all.

The Bed of Jezebel

In Revelation 2:20–22, the Lord rebukes the church in Thyatira:

> *"Because thou sufferest that woman Jezebel, which calleth herself a prophetess, to teach and to seduce my servants... behold, I will cast her into a bed, and them that commit adultery with her into great tribulation..."*

Jezebel invites prophets to her bed.

That "bed" is a place of compromise, of mixture, of shared secrets and corrupted intimacy. It is where prophetic purity dies — not by force, but by seduction.

Once you lie with Jezebel, you lose the right to confront her.

You may still speak — but Heaven will no longer echo your voice.

Prophets for Hire

Just as Balaam was hired to curse what God had blessed (Numbers 22–24), so today there are prophets for hire.

They will say:

"You will be blessed."

"This is your season."

"Breakthrough is coming."

"God says increase."

But they will not say:

"Repent."

"Tear down your idols."

"The fire is coming."

"You are in sin."

Because that doesn't sell.

The prophetic has become an industry, and Jezebel is the CEO.

She trains her prophets to be pleasant, polished, and profitable.

But not holy.

What True Prophets Look Like

A true prophet:

Weeps before he speaks

Burns before he preaches

Trembles when the word comes

Fears God more than rejection

Speaks fire even if it costs everything Jeremiah tried to keep silent, but the word was like a fire in his bones.

Isaiah said, "Woe is me" before he said "Woe to them."

John the Baptist lived in the wilderness — not on stage.

Jesus — the greatest Prophet — was rejected in His own town and crucified in Jerusalem.

True prophets rarely go viral.

But they move Heaven.

A Remnant Must Arise

It is time for a cleansing of the prophetic office.

The Lord is calling:

> Watchmen back to the wall
>
> Prophets back to the secret place
>
> Messengers back to the fire
>
> Voices back to the wilderness

There is a generation of holy, nameless, fearless prophets rising.

They will not eat Jezebel's food.

They will not drink Babylon's wine.

They will not bow to cultural altars.

They will speak what the Lord says — even if no one listens.

Final Reflection

Prophets who sleep with Jezebel will be judged with her.
They may prosper now.
They may be featured, followed, and praised.
But when the fire comes, only what is holy will remain.
The Spirit is speaking to the Church once again:

> *"I gave her space to repent... but she repented not..."*

Let the prophets return.
Let the altars be rebuilt.
Let the fire of truth burn again.
For the mouth of the Lord has spoken it.

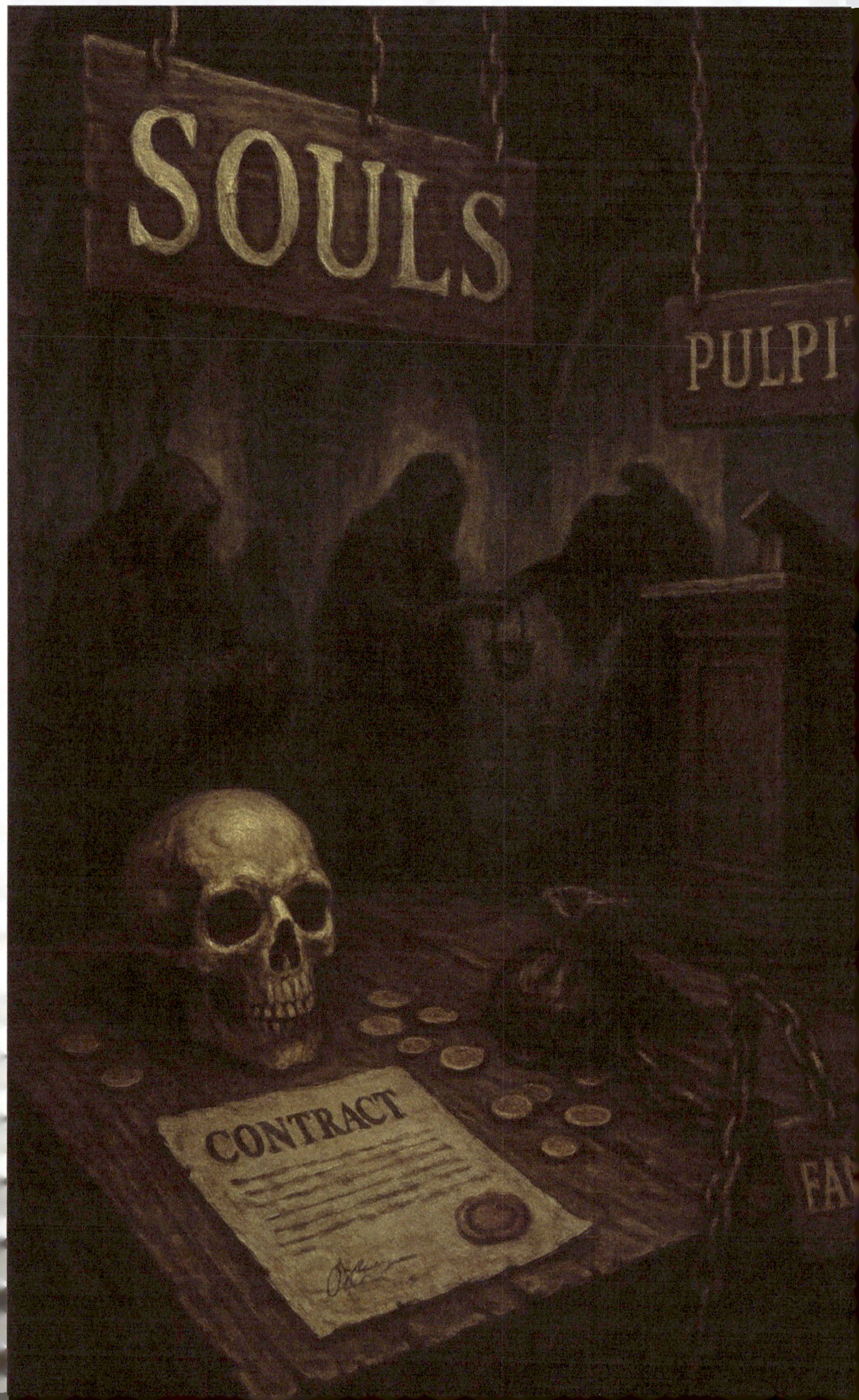
SOULS
PULPI
CONTRACT

Chapter Six
Trading in Souls — The Economics of the Harlot

She has always been a merchant.

Babylon may dress like a queen and speak like a prophetess, but her true business is trade — and her most profitable commodity has always been the human soul.

> *"And the merchants of the earth shall weep and mourn over her; for no man buyeth their merchandise any more...fine flour, wheat, beasts, sheep, horses, chariots, and slaves, and souls of men..."*
> *(Revelation 18:11–13 KJV)*

She sells what should never be sold.

She markets what should remain sacred.

She turns hearts into currency and worship into product.

Babylon does not just seduce. She transacts.

The Marketplace of Mixture

From the Garden to the last generation, Satan's strategy has always been to turn covenants into contracts.

He takes what is holy and makes it marketable.

He takes what is priceless and puts it on a shelf.

Babylon's economy is built on:

Manipulated desire

Religious performance

Consumerism dressed in spirituality

The illusion of access to God — at a price

She learned this from her ancient mothers:

From Egypt's enslavement of bodies, to Tyre's trading of gold and gems (Ezekiel 27), to Rome's taxation of the saints — Babylon now refines it into a global spiritual business.

The Church as a Marketplace

"When Jesus entered the Temple and saw the moneychangers, He overturned their tables and drove them out with a whip..." (John 2:14–16 KJV)

Why?

Because they had turned worship into economy.

Today, the same tables remain:

Prophetic words for sale

Healing conferences with ticket tiers

VIP access to "anointing rooms"

Churches that operate more like franchises than families "Sow a seed to receive your miracle" programs.

These are not isolated errors — they are Babylon's systems, alive and accepted.

The house of prayer has become a house of profit, and the Lord is preparing His whip again.

The Souls of Men

Let us not miss the horror of Revelation 18:13.

The final items listed in Babylon's marketplace are not spices or animals.

They are slaves, and souls.

This is more than physical slavery — it is the capturing of will, identity, and spirit through: Addictive digital platforms.

Spiritually manipulative teaching.

False promises of healing or success.

Cultural systems that reduce people to units of productivity or targets of manipulation.

Babylon's economy does not need to chain your body if it can enslave your mind.

She traffics in false promises, fear-based control, and religious manipulation.

And she does it in the name of God.

The Seduction of Success

One of the most successful products Babylon sells is "Christian success."

It comes wrapped in:

Big stages

Best-selling books

Branded ministries

Airbrushed testimonies

Manufactured "moves of God"

It is often preached as destiny, purpose, calling, favor — but it is success on Babylon's terms, not God's.

The result?

A generation chasing a version of Jesus who gives crowns without crosses.

The True Economy of the Kingdom

The Kingdom of God has its own economy.

It is built not on buying and selling, but on giving and dying.

The currency is obedience.

The investment is sacrifice.

The reward is righteousness.

The offering is your life.

Jesus said, "You cannot serve God and mammon." (Matthew 6:24)

Babylon says, "Why not both?"

But the cross does not negotiate.

You cannot carry the cross and carry Babylon's wallet at the same time.

A Righteous Remnant Must Resist

In every generation, God raises up those who refuse to sell out.

They cannot be bought with platform or money.

They will not market the anointing.

They do not traffic in souls.

They are stewards — not sellers.

These are the ones who flip tables, tear down false systems, and build altars instead of empires.

Their names may not trend.

But their lives are written in Heaven.

Final Reflection

Babylon is still trading.

She has customers in every nation, partners in every system, and

sellers in every sanctuary.

But the voice from Heaven is clear:

> *"Come out of her, My people,*
> *that ye be not partakers of her sins,*
> *and that ye receive not of her plagues...*
> *(Revelation 18:4 KJV)*

The time to buy and sell is ending.

The fire is coming.

Let the marketplaces fall.

Let the souls be freed.

Let the Bride cleanse her hands.

For the Bridegroom is not returning for a merchant—He is

returning for a pure, burning, faithful Bride.

Chapter Seven
The False Light — Her Religion in the Name of Unity and Peace

She no longer demands that the world bow through war.

She now whispers, "Let us be one."

She no longer invades with swords — she invites with songs.

Her newest disguise is her most dangerous yet:

A religion of light.

A gospel of peace.

A unity without the Cross.

Babylon's daughters do not always appear vile.

They are not always clothed in crimson.

Many now wear white, speak of love, and offer a gospel so inclusive it no longer saves.

This is the false light —a seductive system of spiritual compromise masked as enlightenment, tolerance, and progress.

A Gospel with No Offense

The true Gospel offends the flesh.

It calls sinners to repent.

It divides truth from error.

It puts the Cross before the crown.

But Babylon's daughters offer another way — a gentler, broader road:

"We're all children of God."

"Every path leads to the same source."

"God accepts you just as you are — no need to change."

"Jesus is love — He wouldn't judge anyone."

It sounds sweet.

It sounds peaceful.

It is death.

This is not the Gospel. It is a counterfeit, forged in Babylon's furnace.

The Religion of the End-Times Harlot

John saw it in his vision: a woman clothed in outward glory, with a cup in her hand and a name on her forehead — Mystery.

She had form but no faith.

She had ritual but no righteousness.

She represents a worldwide religious system — global, unifying, beautiful on the outside — but full of abominations within.

This system:

Preaches inclusion without transformation.

Elevates spirituality without submission.

Celebrates morality without holiness.

Unites denominations, faiths, ideologies — all without repentance.

Her light is not Heaven's light.

It is a false dawn — a glow that comforts but never convicts.

And she is welcomed with open arms.

Interfaith Altars and Ecumenical Smoke

The world is being prepared for a one-world religion — not through terror, but through peaceful deception.

Interfaith services where Christ is merely "one of many"

Political gatherings with prayers to "the divine, whoever you are"

Church leaders embracing false religions "for unity's sake"

Christian artists collaborating with spiritualists for "higher inspiration"

It is all cloaked in love — but it is the love of Delilah, stroking the hair of the strong while preparing them for slaughter.

This is the altar of false unity —where the name of Jesus is spoken, but His authority is denied.

Her Peace Is Not His Peace

Jesus said,

> *"Think not that I am come to send peace on earth: I came*
> *not to send peace, but a sword..."*
> *(Matthew 10:34 KJV)*

The sword He spoke of was not violence — it was division between truth and error, light and darkness, the holy and the profane.

Babylon's peace has no sword.

It demands no decision.

It promises heaven but never mentions hell.

It offers community, but not covenant.

It gathers people, but does not sanctify them.

Her peace is the kind that dulls the conscience and soothes rebellion.

Her light blinds rather than reveals.

And millions follow it.

The True Light Always Exposes

The true light of Christ reveals sin.

It confronts lies.

It cuts through every false peace with the precision of truth.

> *"Paul warned that Satan himself masquerades as an angel of light..."*
> *(2 Corinthians 11:14 KJV)*

He doesn't always come with horns — sometimes he comes with a smile and a robe.

Babylon's daughters have inherited this masquerade.

They host revivals with no repentance.

They release music with no message.

They write books that inspire the soul but never transform it.

This is not the light of the Lamb—this is the glow of Babylon's religion.

Let the Bride Discern the Light

In the last days, even the elect would be deceived if possible (Matthew 24:24).

And the greatest deception is not in darkness — it is in false light.

The Bride must sharpen her discernment.

She must ask:

Does this message align with Scripture?

Is this light exposing sin or just flattering the flesh?

Does this worship lead me to the Cross — or to my own desires?

Is this unity rooted in Christ, or in comfort?

The Spirit of the Lord is once again dividing wheat from chaff, sheep from goats, light from light.

Only one will remain.

Final Reflection

The religion of Babylon is gentle, inclusive, affirming—

and damning.

Her daughters glow with tolerance but burn with rebellion.

They reject the Cross while building towers to heaven.

They unify nations around a gospel with no Christ.

But the voice of the Spirit still cries out:

> *"Come out of her, My people..."*
> *"Not just from the darkness —*
> *but from the false light..."*

Let the true light shine again.

Let the fire of holiness burn.

Let the Bride walk in the clarity of the Lamb.

For Babylon's glow is fading.

And the true Light is about to break the sky.

HEAVEN
ON
DEMAND

Chapter Eight
Doctrines of Devils — From the Tower to the Temple

There is a theology being preached today that Hell never authored — but neither did Heaven.

It is not human error or cultural drift.

It is demonic design.

The Apostle Paul warned:

> *"Now the Spirit speaketh expressly, that in the latter times some shall depart from the faith, giving heed to seducing spirits, and doctrines of devils..."*
> *(1 Timothy 4:1 KJV)*

These are not innocent misunderstandings.

These are strategies from the pit — disguised as revelation, dressed in light, and planted in pulpits.

They began at a tower in Babel.

They now sit in the temple.

And their mission is singular:

To destroy the pure faith from the inside out.

The Tower of Self

Babel was not just architecture — it was a doctrine.

> *"Let us build us a city... and a tower, whose top may reach unto heaven; and let us make us a name..."*
> *(Genesis 11:4 KJV)*

It was a theology of:

> Human power without divine direction
>
> Unity without truth
>
> Worship without obedience

Babylon has taken this same doctrine and renamed it:

> "Manifest your destiny."
>
> "You are your own breakthrough."
>
> "You're enough."
>
> "Live your truth."

This is not Christian encouragement. It is the gospel of self.

It exalts man, demotes God, and removes repentance.

It has no room for surrender — only success.

From Pyramids to Platforms

What began in Babel's bricks is now broadcast in high-definition.

False doctrines have become content, branding, and networks.

Today's doctrines of devils sound like:

> "Jesus died so you can be rich."
>
> "The anointing guarantees influence."
>
> "If you have enough faith, you'll never suffer."
>
> "God is always pleased — even in your rebellion."
>
> "Hell is just a metaphor."
>
> "Everyone will be saved eventually."

Each of these is a seed from the serpent.

They do not free the soul — they bind it with velvet chains.

Seducing Spirits in Christian Language

The danger is not in the obvious. It's in the almost.

Satan does not always deny truth — he twists it.

He doesn't say, "God doesn't love you." He says, "God loves you too much to discipline you."

He doesn't say, "Jesus didn't rise." He says, "Jesus rose, but your truth matters more."

He doesn't say, "There is no hell." He says, "God wouldn't send anyone there."

And so, the Church drinks from the cup of almost-Gospel, never realizing it has become a house of mixture.

From the Temple to TikTok

Doctrines of devils don't only live in books or sermons — they live in social streams, in songs, in 15-second reels that carry 15 generations of deception.

What once took generations to erode now happens in a scroll.

Entire generations are discipled by false teaching with trending sounds.

Reels that mock holiness.

Music that glorifies sin while naming Jesus

Influencers who offer prophetic coaching but haven't opened a Bible in years.

The Tower has now entered the Temple of the algorithm.

And Babylon is trending.

Doctrines That Kill

Some of the most popular teachings today are killing souls:

Universalism — "Everyone will be saved, no matter what."

Hyper-grace — "Repentance is unnecessary. God already sees you as perfect."

New Age Christianity — "Speak it, claim it, manifest it — you are divine."

Anti-Israel theology — "The Church has replaced God's covenant with Israel."

Jesus without judgment — "God doesn't judge. That's old-fashioned."

Each one chips away at truth.

Each one dulls the sword.

Each one leads the sheep closer to the cliff.

And still, people say "Amen."

The Temple Must Be Cleansed

Jesus overturned tables.

He also cast out doctrine.

When Peter rebuked Him for speaking of the Cross, Jesus said:

> *"Get thee behind me, Satan..." (Matthew 16:23 KJV)*

He didn't call Peter Satan — He rebuked the doctrine behind the voice.

We must do the same.

It's time to:

Test every spirit

Tear down every high thing that exalts itself

Refuse to follow teachers who feed the flesh

Return to the pure doctrine of Christ

The Bride must know the difference between what is popular and what is true.

Final Reflection

The Tower still stands — not in bricks, but in books.

The Temple is infiltrated — not with idols, but with ideologies.

And the Lord is still cleansing.

Let every doctrine that denies the Cross be cast out.

Let every preacher who peddles poison be exposed.

Let every soul be awakened.

For Babylon's teachings are not new.

They are ancient, seductive, and damning.

But the Sword still divides.

The Word still stands.

And the fire still purifies.

Let the Bride return to the altar of truth.

Let the Temple be filled with glory again.

Chapter Nine
Zion or Babylon? Discerning the Bride from the Impostor

Two women walk the pages of Scripture.

One is radiant, pure, clothed in fine linen — prepared for her Husband.

The other is seductive, proud, drunk with power — riding a beast with a cup full of filth.

One is the Bride of Christ.

The other is Babylon the Great.

They both speak.

They both worship.

They both claim love.

But only one wears white in truth.

The greatest deception in the last days will not be Satan as darkness, but Babylon dressed as the Church.

We are no longer deciding between the world and the Cross.

We are deciding between Zion and Babylon — and many don't know the difference.

The Bride Is Hidden, Babylon Is Loud

Babylon parades herself.

She boasts of her achievements. She flaunts her wealth. She seduces kings and sits on platforms.

Zion, by contrast, is humble.

She is found in hidden places —

prayer rooms, wildernesses, upper rooms.

She prepares herself not with spectacle, but with oil.

> *"And to her was granted that she should be arrayed in fine linen, clean and white:*
> *for the fine linen is the righteousness of saints..."*
> *(Revelation 19:8 KJV)*

Zion is preparing.

Babylon is performing.

Babylon Uses the Name of Jesus — But Denies His Lordship

The most dangerous part of Babylon's deception is that she knows the name.

She references Jesus.

She sings songs to Him.

She preaches His blessings.

But she does not submit.

She does not tremble.

She does not repent.

She calls Him Savior, but not Lord.

She declares the Cross, but will not carry it.

She wears the garments of a bride, but sleeps with the kings of the earth.

Her gospel is wide.

Her altar is gold.

But her heart is corrupt.

How to Tell the Difference

The Bride and the Harlot both operate in the visible Church — but the difference is in the fruit, the fire, and the foundation.

1. The Fruit

    Zion bears holiness, humility, and hunger for truth

    Babylon bears pride, mixture, and self-exaltation

2. The Fire

    Zion is refined by suffering

    Babylon avoids the fire and fakes the anointing

3. The Foundation

    Zion builds on Christ, the Rock

    Babylon builds on man's ambition, charisma, and control

You will know them not by their appearance,

but by their allegiance.

The Harlot Imitates the Bride

Babylon is a master of mimicry.

> *"She imitates worship, She imitates holiness,*
> *She imitates community, She imitates even miracles..."*
> *(Revelation 13:13–14 KJV)*

> *"But it is all imitation — absent of covenant..."*
> *"She offers a form of godliness, but denies its power..."*
> *(2 Timothy 3:5 KJV)*

She uses the language of love, but knows nothing of the Cross.

She builds a temple — but places herself on the throne.

And in the end, she will sit where only the Bride was meant to stand.

The Bride Must Discern

This is the hour of separation.

The Lord is not returning for a divided bride, or a deceived bride.

He is returning for a pure, spotless, prepared Bride who knows His voice and lives in His truth.

To be that Bride, we must:

Reject every seductive gospel

Flee every form of spiritual adultery

Embrace the refining fire

Love righteousness more than relevance

Walk in holiness even when the world laughs

We must choose the wilderness over the throne,

the altar over the stage,

the bridegroom over Babylon.

Final Reflection

Zion or Babylon?

It is the choice before every believer.

Every pastor.

Every nation.

Every church.

One leads to a wedding.

The other, to fire.

One sings, "Worthy is the Lamb."

The other cries, "I sit as queen and shall see no sorrow."

But judgment is coming.

And only one will endure.

Let the Bride arise.

Let her cleanse her garments.

Let her lift her eyes to the hills — for the King is coming.

And He knows who is truly His.

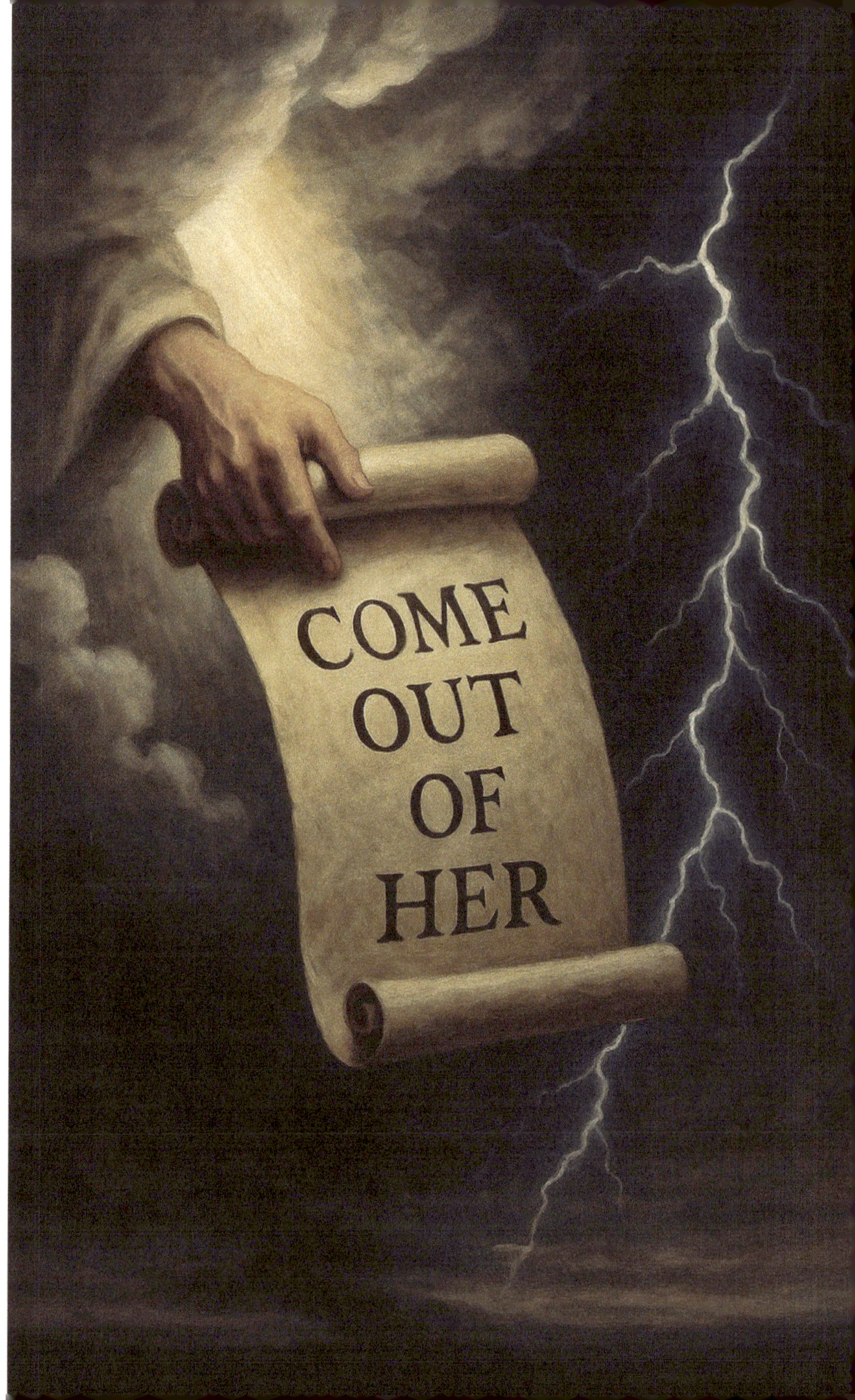
COME
OUT
OF
HER

Chapter Ten
The Call to Come Out — Still Echoing

It was not whispered.

It thundered.

A voice from Heaven — not from earth, not from man, not from religion — pierced the judgment scene of Revelation 18 with one final command:

> *"Come out of her, My people,*
> *that ye be not partakers of her sins,*
> *and that ye receive not of her plagues..."*
> *(Revelation 18:4 KJV)*

This is not just a warning for ancient Israel.

This is not only a message to pagans.

This is a direct call to the people of God —because some of God's people are still inside Babylon's house.

The harlot has daughters, and those daughters have pews.

They host conferences.

They produce worship albums.

They write devotionals.

And the Lord is still speaking.

> *"Come out of her."*

God's People Are in Dangerous Places

The tragedy of the modern Church is not that darkness exists — it's that many believers live in it and call it light.

They sit under compromised preaching

They partner with systems rooted in corruption

They sing with voices that do not know the fire.

They defend leaders God has already judged.

They cry out, "Grace!"

And the Lord cries out, "Get out."

It is not an invitation — it is a rescue.

If we do not come out of Babylon, Babylon will come into us.

Come Out of Her Religion

Many think Babylon is just a city or a political empire — but the Harlot's greatest stronghold is religion.

The Spirit is saying:

Come out of counterfeit worship

Come out of prophetic manipulation

Come out of charismatic showmanship

Come out of grace that costs nothing

Come out of holiness that never confronts sin

Religion without repentance is not revival — it is Babylon dressed for Sunday.

Come Out of Her Economics

Babylon's daughters build empires on offerings.

They market the anointing.

They turn the sheep into customers.

If your walk with God is measured by how much you give, how

much you earn, how many views you get —you are not in Zion.

You are in Babylon.

The Church is not a brand.

The Cross is not a slogan.

The altar is not a platform.

The time to come out is now.

Come Out of Her Politics

Babylon seduces kings — and she seduces churches that want to be close to power.

She offers religious leaders:

Access

Prestige

Influence

Partnerships

Favor from Pharaoh

But those who dine with Babylon's kings often lose the right to speak for Heaven's King.

When spiritual leaders refuse to speak against sin to preserve access to earthly thrones —they have already committed adultery with the Harlot.

Come out.

Come Out of Her Platforms

This is perhaps the most painful:

Babylon's daughters dominate the modern platform.

They own the algorithm.

They fund the festivals.

They host the influencers.

They polish the image of a gospel that no longer saves.

But the Lord does not anoint platforms. He anoints altars.

If your identity is built on visibility rather than obedience.

If your fire dies when your platform shrinks.

You may be more entangled in Babylon than you know.

Come out.

This Call Is Urgent

"Come out of her..."

Why?

"That you be not partakers of her sins..."
"...and that you receive not of her plagues..."

The plagues are coming.

The judgment is sure.

Babylon will fall — quickly, violently, permanently.

And anyone still in her house —

whether by compromise, complacency, or fear —

will fall with her.

This is mercy speaking.

This is love warning.

This is the Bridegroom shouting through the storm:

Come out, beloved. The door is closing.

Final Reflection

There is still time.

But not much.

The Spirit and the Bride do not say, "Stay."

They say, "Come."

Come out of the noise.

Come out of the mixture.

Come out of the systems.

Come out of the spotlight.

Come out of the lies.

Come into the wilderness.

Come into the truth.

Come into the fire.

Come into the presence of the Lamb.

For Babylon is falling.

And Zion is rising.

Let the Bride hear.

Let the Bride obey.

Let the Bride come out.

Chapter Eleven
The Bride Without Mixture — Holy, Watching, Ready

She is not loud.

She does not seduce.

She does not ride beasts or drink from golden cups.

She does not mingle light with darkness or truth with lies.

She is the Bride of Christ — and she is without mixture.

In an age of compromise, she remains consecrated.

In a world of performance, she stays pure.

While Babylon's daughters build thrones and brand ministries,

the Bride is found in the secret place, preparing.

She is not perfect by the world's standards — but she is holy,

for she walks in obedience, in repentance, and in fear of the Lord.

This is the remnant.

This is the Bride.

The Bride Has One Husband

> *"For I am jealous over you with godly jealousy: for I have espoused you to one husband,*
> *that I may present you as a chaste virgin to Christ."*
> *(2 Corinthians 11:2 KJV)*

The true Bride is not married to Babylon.

She is not in covenant with the world.

She is not flirting with Jezebel or entertaining the Harlot.

She is betrothed — set apart — to One.

Her desire is for the Bridegroom, not the crowd.

Her goal is not influence — it is intimacy.

While Babylon's daughters chase kings,

the Bride waits for the King of kings.

Without Mixture

What does it mean to be without mixture?

It means preaching truth, even when it costs you followers.

It means worshipping in spirit and in truth, not in performance and sound.

It means refusing to mix holiness with hype, righteousness with relevance, or Scripture with sentiment.

It means no longer drinking from Babylon's cup, even if everyone else does.

The Bride does not blend in.

She stands out — because she refuses to blend truth with error.

She walks the narrow path.

She trims her lamp.

She guards her oil.

Watching

Jesus told of ten virgins — all waiting for the Bridegroom, all holding lamps.

But only five were watching wisely, and only five had oil.

> *"Watch therefore, for ye know neither the day nor the hour wherein the Son of man cometh..."*
> *(Matthew 25:13 KJV)*

The Bride is awake.

She discerns the hour.

She listens for footsteps.

She watches the skies and searches her heart.

She is not distracted by Babylon's lights or seduced by her sounds.

She is watching — not scrolling.

Her eyes are not on the beast, but on the Bridegroom.

Ready

The Church is not only called to love Christ —

She is called to prepare herself.

> *"And his wife hath made herself ready..."*
> *(Revelation 19:7 KJV)*

The Bride is not passive.

She washes her robes.

She lays down sin.

She prays without ceasing.

She loves truth even when it wounds.

She embraces the Cross without conditions.

She does not wait to be purified by pressure —She chooses to be refined by fire.

She is ready, not because of ease, but because of surrender.

The Separation Is Now

Babylon is not waiting.

She is active — preaching, seducing, infiltrating.

But so is the Spirit.

He is cleansing, calling, separating.

The final separation is not coming someday — it is already underway.

Those who carry mixture will be exposed.

Those who carry oil will be preserved.

Those who cling to Babylon will fall.

Those who remain in Christ will rise.

Let every heart ask:

Am I the Bride... or just a guest at the wedding?

Final Reflection

She is almost ready.

Her garments are white.

Her lamp is lit.

Her eyes are lifted.

Her spirit is burning.

The Bride is not blending — she is becoming.

She is not apologizing — she is arising.

While Babylon builds cities, she is building altars.

While Babylon gathers kings, she waits for the only Crown that matters.

Let the Bride be holy.

Let her be without mixture.

Let her watch.

Let her be ready.

For the cry will come at midnight...

"Behold, the Bridegroom cometh..."

And only those who prepared will enter in.

Chapter Twelve
The Spirit and the Bride Say Come — The Last Invitation Before the Door Shuts

There is a voice rising in the earth.

It is not Babylon's voice.

It is not the voice of religion or politics or culture.

It is the voice of the Spirit.

And it is in harmony with the voice of the Bride.

Together, they are crying out:

> *"And the Spirit and the Bride say, Come.*
> *And let him that heareth say, Come.*
> *And let him that is athirst come.*
> *And whosoever will, let him take the water of life freely..."*
> *(Revelation 22:17 KJV)*

This is the final call,

the last invitation before the door shuts,

before the Bridegroom returns,

before Babylon falls into fire.

It is mercy.

It is urgency.

It is love with tears in its voice.

And it will not be open forever.

The Cry of the Spirit

The Holy Spirit is not passive in the last days.

He is not silent or confused.

He is not adapting to culture — He is convicting it.

The Spirit is:

Exposing the false

Uncovering the mixture

Awakening the remnant

Drawing the hungry

Warning the compromised

Preparing the Bride

He groans with intercession.

He baptizes with fire.

He calls us out of Babylon — not with condemnation, but with urgency and clarity.

"Come..."
Not later.
Not someday.
Now.

The Cry of the Bride

The Bride, too, is crying.

She has seen too much deception.

She has endured too much mixture.

She has waited too long in the wilderness.

Now she cries, "Come!"

Come, Lord Jesus.

Come quickly.

Come judge the earth with righteousness.

Come purify the nations.

Come redeem the righteous blood spilled.

Come rule and reign.

The cry of the Bride is not selfish.

It is not escapism.

It is longing for justice, for holiness, for final union with her King.

She is ready — and she is calling others to be ready too.

The Final Invitation

The gospel is not just for the clean — it is for the thirsty.

"Let him that is athirst come..."
"Whosoever will, let him take the water of life freely..."

Even now — after Babylon has seduced, after the Harlot has ruled–

God still offers water.

Still opens the door.

Still says, "Come."

To the compromised — come.

To the weary — come.

To the proud — come.

To the deceived — come.

To the ashamed — come.

He is not calling perfect people — He is calling people who are

willing to leave Babylon behind.

But the Door Will Shut

Every invitation has a time limit.

Every mercy has a window.

Jesus told the parable of the wedding feast (Matthew 25) —those

who were ready entered in.

But those who were late... found the door shut.

They knocked.

They begged.

They even called Him "Lord."

But the answer was final:

"I know you not..."

This is not cruelty — it is justice.

Those who refused the invitation while it was open

will not be permitted when it closes.

This is the season of invitation.

But it will not last forever.

Let Him That Heareth Say, "Come"

This is the mandate of the faithful.

It is not enough to hear the cry — we must echo it.

Let pastors cry, "Come."

Let prophets cry, "Come."

Let worshippers cry, "Come."

Let missionaries, teachers, elders, children —

Let all who hear Heaven's voice become Heaven's voice.

We must no longer call people to church attendance — we must call them to Christ.

We must no longer call people to safety — we must call them to surrender.

The Spirit is moving.

The Bride is speaking.

The earth is shaking.

And the echo must multiply.

Final Reflection

This is the last chapter of invitation.

After this comes the Wedding.

After this comes the fire.

After this comes the King with eyes like flames.

But today — there is still time.

Today — the door is still open.

Today — the Spirit still speaks.

Today — the Bride still waits.

And the cry remains:

"Come."

Come out of her.

Come into Him.

Come before the door shuts.

For the Spirit has spoken.

The Bride has responded.

And the King is coming.

Conclusion
Fire and Glory — The Fall of the Harlot and the Rise of the Lamb

There is only one way Babylon's story ends:

With fire.

> *"Therefore shall her plagues come in one day, death, and mourning, and famine;*
> *and she shall be utterly burned with fire: for strong is the Lord God who judgeth her..."*
> *(Revelation 18:8 KJV)*

No matter how rich her garments…

No matter how loud her music…

No matter how powerful her alliances…

She will fall.

Not by human rebellion.

Not by political reform.

But by the sovereign judgment of a holy God.

And her daughters —those systems and spirits who carried her name, mimicked her seduction, and drank from her cup —will fall with her.

Babylon Ends in Ashes

The merchants will weep.

The kings will mourn.

The nations will tremble.

But Heaven will rejoice.

> *"Rejoice over her, thou heaven, and ye holy apostles and*
> *prophets; for God hath avenged you on her..."*
> *(Revelation 18:20 KJV)*

For every prophet silenced…

For every saint martyred…

For every altar desecrated…

For every soul deceived…

There will be justice.

Babylon's fire is not random — it is righteous.

And the Lamb Will Rise

From the ashes of the great Harlot's fall,

another sound breaks forth — a greater sound:

> *"Let us be glad and rejoice, and give honour to him:*
> *for the marriage of the Lamb is come, and his wife hath*
> *made herself ready..." (Revelation 19:7 KJV)*

She is not clothed in crimson — but in white.

She is not drunk with the blood of saints — but washed by it.

She is not seated on a beast — but walking with the Bridegroom.

The Bride.

Holy.

Spotless.

Burning with oil.

Covered in glory.

Prepared.

While Babylon builds cities that crumble, the Bride has built an altar

that cannot be shaken.

And now, she is ready.

This Is Where It Ends — And Begins

This book is not about Babylon's story.
It is about choosing who you belong to.
You are either drinking from her cup
or drinking from His.
You are either clothed in her colors
or clothed in His righteousness.
You are either building her house
or waiting for His return.
There is no third option.
There is no neutral path.
There is no delay left.
This is not just a message — it is a summons.

A Final Call

Let every pastor return to truth.
Let every prophet be purified by fire.
Let every worshipper cast down idols.
Let every saint trim their lamp.
Let every soul come out of her.
Babylon is falling.
Zion is rising.
The Bride is readying.
The King is coming.
And the Spirit still speaks:
"Come."
Let the nations hear.
Let the Church awaken.
Let the Bride arise.
The fire will fall.
But after the fire…
The glory will remain.

Scripture Index
Verses cited throughout Babylon's Daughters: The Legacy of Seduction in the Nations

Revelation

Glossary of Key Terms

Babylon (Mystery Babylon)

A prophetic symbol from the Book of Revelation referring not only to a historical empire, but to a spiritual system of corruption, seduction, false religion, and global control. Babylon represents the antithesis of the pure Bride of Christ and is described as the "Mother of Harlots" (Revelation 17:5).

The Harlot

A biblical figure in Revelation symbolizing a false religious system that is outwardly glorious but inwardly full of idolatry and spiritual adultery. She is seen riding a beast and drinking from a cup of abominations. She typifies religious mixture and compromise with worldly powers.

The Bride (of Christ)

The true Church — holy, consecrated, and prepared for union with Christ at His return. She is described in Revelation as clothed in white linen, without spot or wrinkle, having made herself ready for the marriage of the Lamb (Revelation 19:7–8).

Mixture

The spiritual condition in which truth is combined with error, holiness with compromise, or the Gospel with worldly ideologies. It is the defining trait of Babylon's influence and the very thing the Bride must be cleansed from.

The Cup (of Babylon)

A golden cup in the hand of the Harlot filled with abominations and the blood of saints (Revelation 17:4, 6). Symbolically represents seduction, deception, and participation in false worship and religious compromise.

The Beast

In Revelation, a political and spiritual power system that carries and supports the Harlot. Represents the alignment of worldly governments and false religion.

Jezebel (Spirit of)

A spirit of seduction and control that corrupts prophetic voices and leads God's servants into compromise. Referenced both in the Old Testament (1 Kings 16–21) and prophetically in Revelation 2:20, where the church is warned for tolerating her.

Doctrines of Devils

Teachings that are inspired by demonic deception rather than the Holy Spirit (1 Timothy 4:1). They include spiritual distortions, false gospels, hyper-grace without repentance, and ideologies that deny the Lordship of Christ.

The Remnant

A faithful, purified portion of God's people who remain consecrated in the midst of widespread deception and apostasy. The remnant refuses to bow to Babylon or Jezebel and longs for the return of the true King.

The Bridegroom

A title for Jesus Christ, emphasizing His coming return for a prepared Bride — the Church. The imagery is drawn from Jewish wedding traditions and reflects the relationship between Christ and His people.

Come Out of Her

A divine command from Revelation 18:4 calling God's people to separate themselves from Babylon's spiritual, religious, and cultural systems in order to avoid her judgment.

False Light

A form of deception that appears spiritual or righteous on the surface but leads people away from truth. Often manifests through false unity, counterfeit love, and religious activity devoid of true holiness.

The Altar

A place of consecration, sacrifice, and surrender to God. In contrast to Babylon's stage and platform, the altar represents true spiritual worship and the fire of purification.

Watchmen

Prophetic voices positioned to see, warn, and call the people of God to repentance. Watchmen do not entertain — they cry out.

Oil (of the Wise Virgins)

Symbolic of the Holy Spirit and intimacy with God. Found in the parable of the ten virgins (Matthew 25), the oil represents spiritual readiness, prayer, purity, and constant connection to the Bridegroom.

The Fire

Refers to God's refining, purifying presence — both in this age and in judgment. It burns away mixture, exposes what is false, and prepares the Bride for glory.

Biblical Commentaries & Theological Works

Matthew Henry, Commentary on the Whole Bible

John Gill, Exposition of the Old and New Testaments

Charles Spurgeon, Sermons on Revelation and Holiness

Derek Prince, Foundations for Christian Living

Leonard Ravenhill, Why Revival Tarries

David Wilkerson, The Vision and Beyond

Watchman Nee, The Normal Christian Life

A.W. Tozer, The Knowledge of the Holy

Dietrich Bonhoeffer, The Cost of Discipleship

Historical and Prophetic Resources

Josephus, The Antiquities of the Jews

Eusebius, Church History

Foxe's Book of Martyrs

Church records and writings from the early Patristic Fathers

Firsthand study of revival history, the persecuted Church, and

political-religious alliances across church history

Academic & Cultural References

Hannah Arendt, The Origins of Totalitarianism.

Francis Schaeffer, How Should We Then Live?

OS. Guinness, Prophetic Untimeliness.

Eric Metaxas, Bonhoeffer: Pastor, Martyr, Prophet, Spy.

Studies on Babylonian culture and Mesopotamian worship, Systems Analysis of modern ecumenical movements and interfaith trends.

Sociopolitical commentary on globalism and the moral collapse of Western civilization.

Supplementary Resources

Transcripts and recordings from global prophetic summits.

Intercessory prayer insights from the Global Watchman Network.

Unofficial transcripts of modern apostolic and prophetic teachings for doctrinal comparison.

Internal interviews and private correspondence with underground church leaders and revival intercessors.

About the Author

Damiano B. Centola is a prophetic writer, biblical thinker, and spiritual watchman for this generation. Known for his piercing insight and poetic theology, his works challenge compromise, awaken the remnant, and prepare the Bride of Christ for the return of the King.

His journey as a writer began in journals and secret places, shaped by years of prayer, study, and encounters with the Word of God. Today, he writes with fire in his bones — calling nations to repentance, churches to holiness, and hearts to the altar. His voice is not that of a religious system, but of a consecrated vessel crying out in the wilderness:

"Make straight the way of the Lord."

Damiano has authored numerous books confronting theological error, celebrating the glory of God's sovereignty, and unveiling the prophetic layers hidden within Scripture, sacred design, and human history. His published works include:

The Mother of Corruption: Unveiling Spiritual Corruption from Babylon to Today

God's Sovereignty: Exploring the Divine Rule Over Creation, History, and Eternity

Divine Encounters: Discovering the Depth and Power of God's Names

The Lord Is My Shepherd: A Journey Through Psalm 23 — Meditations on Trust, Hope, and Eternal Love

I Choose the Call: My Daily Anthem of Devotion — A Journey of Faith, Purpose, and Obedience

The Mystery of Mysteries: Decoding the Divine Proportions of the Human Body Through Art, Anatomy, and Sacred Geometry

Jewish Holidays: Jesus Teaches Us Through Sacred Seasons

The Words of Jesus: Unlocking the Lord's Prayer in Aramaic, Greek, and English

YESHUA (ישוע): The Nazarene, the Refugee, the Redeemer

Yeshua the Builder: From Bethlehem to the Baptism

The Bread of Life: A Journey to Bethlehem

Water Jar: Devotions from the Shadows of Scripture

The Mountain Still Speaks, Volume I: Salt, Light, and Fire from the Sermon That Changed the World

The Mountain Still Speaks, Volume II: Still He Speaks — Echoes from the Higher Ground, the Narrow Way, the Secret Life, and the Rock That Stands

Son of Man: The Glory Hidden in Flesh — A Journey Through the Mystery of Yeshua's Most Mysterious Name

The Fall of Babylon: The Blood of Saints and the Cry from the Earth

The Mother of Harlots: Unveiling Spiritual Corruption from Babylon to Today — Revised and Expanded

Babylon's Daughters: The Legacy of Seduction in the Nations

When he's not writing, Damiano continues to study sacred texts, mentor other prophetic voices, and create bold visual works of truth and beauty across multiple languages and cultures. He believes that clarity, holiness, and courage are the highest callings of any generation that dares to follow the Lamb.

He currently resides in Los Angeles with his beloved wife, Feebe — his greatest gift and partner in every divine assignment.

Note on Proportions and Diagrams

The proportions and diagrams presented in this book are intended to illustrate symbolic, theological, and historical insights drawn from Scripture, art, and sacred geometry. While grounded in anatomical and mathematical research, they represent interpretive models rather than clinical or universally precise measurements of the human body. Their purpose is not to claim absolute scientific accuracy but to reveal the patterns by which artists, architects, and theologians have discerned divine order in creation.

www.ingramcontent.com/pod-product-compliance
Lightning Source LLC
Chambersburg PA
CBHW051226120626
46547CB00013B/1521